This Rarely Happens: Said No One Ever

Alexa Alonzo

BookLeaf
Publishing

India | USA | UK

Presentation by *BookLeaf Publishing*

Web: www.bookleafpub.com

E-mail: info@bookleafpub.com

ISBN: 978-93-5744-428-6

First edition 2022

DEDICATION

To everyone who has lost and found themselves
in strange ways...

ACKNOWLEDGEMENT

Gratitude: a word that I look at every single day because, once upon a time, I took it for granted.

This one is for the many people in my life and for my cat, Macklemore, who inspired me to start exercising gratitude. How I wish you could read this because you deserve the world and more than 9 lives, my little furry soulmate. Thank you for being the light of my life.

Many thanks to my therapist, Paola Ramirez, for being gentle and kind to me from the start, especially when I felt like I didn't deserve either of those gestures. Seven months later, it's become clearer and clearer that I do.

I'd really love to thank all the wonderful ladies in my family for granting me grace and acceptance during my lowest moments: my grandma "Bue", my mom Jenny, my sister Isabella, my cousin Azia, and my aunt Ivelisse. You inspire me to acquire all we deserve for all our futures.

To my boyfriend with the most infectious confidence, love, positivity, and zest for life: Thank You, Honey, for accepting, respecting, and supporting me at my lowest. Your glowing, golden spirit has inspired me to be and do my best. Thank you for also nudging me to read "The Power of Now" by Eckhart Tolle; my life changed immediately after reading its Foreword (so Thank You, too, Mr. Tolle!). I hope every woman in this lifetime and the next finds a strong yet gentle man like you to share their life with.

Massive thanks to BookLeaf Publishing, for this wonderful opportunity that I won't ever take for granted.

Big thanks to me, Alexa Alonzo, for not giving up on myself.

Lastly, the biggest Thank You is to God. I'm eternally grateful for God's protection, life lessons, and blessings, including the opportunity to wake up each day.

I won't take any of you for granted for the rest of my days.

PREFACE

Conversation from 2019:

Them:
Wow, you're really committed to that.
You should become a writer or something!

Me:
points to 3 notebooks with a smirk
I mean... Hello???

silence and more smirks

page flipping commences

The Only

Look on with discern
Walk away; this does not
concern
Me. Nope.

Passive

Stare, wonder
Disgust, eye roll
"That's not how I roll"
Eyes bulge
"What is happening?
Is this my reality?"
No girl, it's his
Can you show a little charity?

Look with confusion
Eye roll again
Shake off the delusion

Aggressive

Nosey
But not with a nose
Only I can see
the snooping
You're quite the hound

New Yorker

Look, don't look
Move, don't move
Moving without momentum
Action without the mention
Mention your anxieties
Without moving your mouth
Let your hands do the talking
And your eyes make the sound

Mission

Stare at the something of nothing
Spacing out
Lots of brain matter
With empty thoughts
Nothing matters
Yet lots of matters
to tend to
So my thoughts
I run from
Pen to paper

Accomplished

Waltzing with your eyes
Dancing thoughts
Making moves
From the heart
No choreography
Your eyes lead the way
Shoving away love

The toes of your brain tappin'
Side to side
Like your eyes
What's wanderin'?
Your love compass, or your mind?

Honesty

Moral bankruptcy
No consistency
Lots of withdrawals
Hardly deposits
Souls and hearts
Slowly rotting

Empathy

My mind vegetates
Hard to relate, equate
Where's my heart rate?
Great, I'll go dissipate

Can't connect with you, you, or even me
Life doesn't make sense
C'est la vie
Let it be

Respect

Wonder through the thunder
Brainstorming
If I wonder
I see you, but not you
Yet I ponder
Does it matter? LGBTQ?
A, I don't care
Show me your journey
Through the waves of

Open-Mindedness

Brain is fried
Something is off
I can't even explain
The switch of events
All I can connect
Is not so apparent

The symptoms are real
Painful enough
These circuits don't heal
They tease you like you died
And that's when I knew
This pain was a lie

The Movies

Fools laugh
Fools soak in small views
Fools relax
Leading to wisdom's muse

Curiosity
Hair spins
Check-ins
Noise wins
Zoom in

Back to the roll
No negatives with these photos
Sprint towards good times
Please
Let's develop more
Just like these

The 2

Eyes bulge
Mind is awake
Cries for help
This can't be fake
This can't be fate
Just need some change
Forget the money
Get me a change of pace
Maker is about to break
Down

Hunts (Point)

Look back at it
Walk like ya had it
Suck ya teeth like ya sampled
Women like her? Not ample
Mind moves forward while ya
Stare back
"Atta boy"
And just like her
Ya didn't even know him

Catch

Happiness in the little things
Big hands catch doors about to close
Big mouth open
Teeth glistening
Then coffee stains get settling

An empty seat makes it all better
Space
For a leg spreader
Gotta love trend setters

The 4

Right in front
What seems like young love
Can't face it
Will it come back?

Changes emerge
Afterall
Winter is coming, and so is fall

Spring dances in
So maybe if I wait too
Groundhog will remind me
Of young love's truth

Hit The Breaks

Trips lead to laughter
It's no wonder we
gather, to share
embarrassing stories
Ease the pain thereafter

Trips lead to smiles
Exchanges
Understandings
Standing one moment
Then on someone's lap
Laughing

Direct The Traffic

Long days
Slow gaze
Which direction do you march
without your Waze?

Are you lost?
Re-stammer this phrase
Finding my way
Towards the words to say

What just happened?
Am I trapped?
Did cupid find me
between love's match???

What the... Hello?
Did you see that???
No crutches could stop
These knees from collapse

Toy with it...

Makes sense...
Shades
Fade shade
Shade away
Fade away
Shade

Okay...
Sounds like the poem
Of a naughty girl
At a coffee shop

Van Who In

If these b*tches
Don't get me a coffee,
I'm going to scream...

Listen yeah,
the answers are in alcohol and ice cream
And that's all I know

Borough (Me)

I wanna be recycled
Away in the mountains
Can you
promise me this?

No, I can't!
…What is this? A can of piss?
Write that down!

Breads

No!
I don't wanna pay
For the crackheads
That's not cool
At all
I don't wanna pay them
Fools
That's it
That's all